SCHIRMER
PERFORMANCE
EDITIONS

HAL LEONARD PIANO LIBRARY

BURGMÜLLER
25 PROGRESSIVE STUDIES
Opus 100

Edited by Margaret Otwell

T0066606

Also available:
00296465 Burgmüller: 25 Progressive Studies, Opus 100,
with companion recordings by Margaret Otwell

Additionally, editor Margaret Otwell's recordings of the pieces
in this collection are available for purchase on iTunes.

On the cover:
Unconscious Rivals (1893)
by Sir Lawrence Alma-Tadema
(1836–1912)

© Bridgeman Art Library, Getty Images

ISBN 978-1-4950-0726-2

G. SCHIRMER, *Inc.*

DISTRIBUTED BY
HAL•LEONARD®
CORPORATION
7777 W. BLUEMOUND RD. P.O. BOX 13819 MILWAUKEE, WI 53213

www.musicsalesclassical.com
www.halleonard.com

CONTENTS

HISTORICAL NOTES

JOHANN FRIEDRICH BURGMÜLLER (1806-1874)

Remembered primarily as a composer of French salon music, Johann Friedrich Burgmüller was in fact German, and he seldom receives credit for his most-often-heard work. Johann Friedrich was born in Regensburg, Germany. His father, Johann August Franz Burgmüller (1766-1824), was a composer and music director who founded the Lower Rhine Music Festival in 1818. It continues today and has served as the inspiration for countless other annual music festivals around the world. Johann Friedrich's brother, Norbert, who was also a composer, showed tremendous potential before his premature death at age 26 in 1836.

Johann Friedrich began his musical studies as a child in his hometown. He eventually moved to Kassel to study with composer Louis Spohr (1784-1859). In 1832 he moved to France, settling in Paris. Some sources say that he relocated to Paris to serve as music teacher to the children of King Louis Philippe. It is certain that he was a fine pianist and began to make a name for himself in Paris as a composer of ballet music. His ballet *La Péri*, (not to be confused with the Dukas ballet of the same name) was first performed in Paris in February 1843. An immediate success, it was performed 50 times at the Paris Opera in a span of two and a half years. It opened in St. Petersburg and Moscow in 1844, in Brussels in 1847, and in New York in 1855. Johann Friedrich also collaborated with Flotow on the score of the ballet *Lady Henrietta*. But it is the music he contributed to Adolphe Adam's legendary ballet *Giselle*, the "Valse de Giselle" and the "Peasant Pas de Deux," that is most often heard and the work for which he is often not credited. Théophile Gautier, author of the book of *La Péri*, called Burgmüller's music "...elegant, delicate, full of adroit and lilting melodies which linger in one's memory…"

Johann Friedrich withdrew from public life in 1844 and focused on his teaching. He wrote piano pieces for the Parisian *salons*—drawing rooms, or living rooms, of the aristocratic and wealthy, where educated, cultured people gathered to hear the latest music, poetry, or literature of the day. In the middle of the 19th century the technology did not yet exist to play recorded music in one's home. Playing an instrument was considered an essential part of a complete education, and most people of means owned instruments and were able to play them. Johann Friedrich's music is part of a tremendous volume of music that was written for these players. Just as we are interested in hearing the latest new songs, people of his day were interested in bringing home the latest pieces and playing it on their pianos. His pieces are difficult enough to be interesting, yet easy enough for a good amateur pianist to master.

—*Elaine Schmidt*

PERFORMANCE NOTES

Burgmüller's *25 Easy & Progressive Studies, Opus 100* have been employed to teach lyrical, Romantic style for more than 150 years. Their enduring popularity is a testament to their charm, immediate appeal, and real pedagogical value. This surely was their purpose, although one could imagine that they served equally well as short, poetic offerings of the composer's creative genius at Paris salons where, undoubtedly, many of them were first heard.

Like many students, my first encounter with the works of Burgmüller came through his most renowned study, *L'Arabesque*. Its evocative minor key and graceful, circular wisps of the melodic line, set against a crisp, chordal accompaniment, were irresistible. Far from looking daunting on the page, this short piece invites the student in, making it easy to enter the rich world of expressive playing that so characterizes the Romantic period. Perhaps this is why so many teachers assign this imaginative work to their students as a first study in Romantic style.

The charm of Burgmüller's Opus 100 studies lies in the vibrant musical character of each solo. Imbued with an individual and highly sculpted personality, they are quite similar in style to the short pieces (*Characterstücke*) by his renowned contemporary, Robert Schumann. We do not know whether Burgmüller assigned descriptive titles to these miniatures himself. It is quite possible to imagine a guest at one of the elegant Paris salons where his music was frequently performed remark, upon hearing a familiar and favorite melody, "Ah, *La Gracieuse!*" In any case, the titles are completely appropriate to the character of the music.

These charming and well-crafted pieces disguise their true intent: to teach technique. Each study is devoted to a specific technical skill that, when mastered, enables a student to express the musical character of the piece. Burgmüller cleverly weds the technical goals to the music itself, succinctly distilling them into an effective and enticing composition, so that as students strive toward a polished performance they are hardly aware that they are actually working on technique.

Some General Comments

Pedal

Although a few pedal indications are found in these studies, they do not truly provide sufficient guidance concerning pedal use. So, I have chosen to leave out all pedal references in this edition. My aim in doing so is to encourage teachers and students to discuss pedaling, and experiment with various options before settling on a preferred choice. Given their Romantic style and expressive character, performers may confidently make free use of the damper pedal and *una corda* pedal throughout these studies.

Fingering

The fingerings in this edition are my own personal choices, and I hope others may find them useful. Just as with pedaling, students and teachers should also experiment with alternative fingerings to find a choice that best suits an individual's hand.

Tempo and Metronome Markings

The metronome indications in the score follow the 1903 *Schirmer's Library of Piano Classics* edition, but in some studies a slightly faster or slower tempo might elicite a better interpretation. A chart listing a range of tempos for each study is printed on the following page. Although the original tempo markings may be the ultimate goal, the slower and faster limits suggested in the chart allow for expressive, stylistic performances by students of varying abilities.

Tempo Chart

Title	Suggested mm. Range
La Candeur	♩ = 144-160
L'Arabesque	♩ = 132-152
La Pastorale	♩. = 63-66
La Petite Réunion	♩ = 138-152
Innocence	♩ = 104-112
Progrès	♩ = 120-132
Le Courant Limpide	♩ = 144-176
La Gracieuse	♩ = 92-100
La Chasse	♩. = 120-132
Tendre Fleur	♩ = 116-126
La Bergeronnette	♩ = 116-126
L'Adieu	♩ = 160-176
Consolation	♩ = 138-152
La Styrienne	♩ = 166-176
Ballade	♩. = 80-92
Douce Plainte	♩ = 112-116
La Babillarde	♩. = 66-72
Inquiétude	♩ = 120-138
Ave Maria	♩ = 80-100
La Tarentelle	♩. = 144-160
L'Harmonie des Anges	♩ = 132-152
Barcarolle	♩. = 66-72
Le Retour	♩. = 112-126
L'Hirondelle	♩ = 120-138
Chevaleresque	♩ = 138-152

The Individual Studies

Most students and teachers already know the more popular studies from Opus 100 quite well. *L'Arabesque*, *Ballade*, *La Tarentelle*, *La Chasse*, *Le Retour*, and *Ave Maria* have all found their way into many anthologies and method books over the years, with good reason. Students of all ages regard them as favorite recital material, and teachers often refer to these particular studies as "pupil savers." Little needs to be said, therefore, about these famous studies from Opus 100, but other gems in the collection are worth noting in more detail. Although we hear them performed less frequently, they also have valuable lessons to impart.

La Candeur, *La Pastorale*, *Tendre Fleur*, *Innocence*, and *Douce Plainte* all focus on *legato* playing, and each has an individual melodic style.

La Candeur's melody consists of steady, fluid eighths in the RH, and is accompanied by simple blocked chords in the LH. This is the first study in the book, and so the technical skills needed here are not demanding. *La Pastorale* provides more practice in playing *cantabile* melodies within the gracious framework of a pastoral 6/8 meter. In this study, a two-voice accompaniment is introduced briefly at mm. 11-14.

Innocence provides advancing students with a first study in "pearling *legato*." The fluid 16ths in the RH melody should cascade down effortlessly and smoothly. In *Tendre Fleur*, varied phrase lengths and detailed articulation make more demands on a student's interpretive skills. A gentle, loping phrase made up of short, two- and four-note slurs is answered by a much longer phrase, spun out over four measures, made more expressive by a LH countermelody. This is the first study in Opus 100 that asks students to play two com-plementary melodies simultaneously, in a lyrical duet.

Douce Plainte comes later in the book, and is more mature in style. This exquisite miniature in G minor requires a supple, lyrical interpretation. Its melodic line weaves back and forth between the hands and needs careful shaping. Due attention must also be given to the short, 16th-note motives that accompany the melody. These subdued, expressive motives call to mind fragile trembling. Like Schumann's "First Loss" from his *Album For The Young*, this solo makes good use of ever-heightened dramatic tension, coming to a poignant climax at the highest point of the melody, and then falling off rapidly to a quiet ending.

Well-defined articulation and rhythmic precision in double notes or scales in tenths, respectively, mark *La Petite Réunion* and *Progrès*, both of which are found in the first half of the book. They are excellent choices to illustrate the difference between a metrical accent and syncopation. They also focus on developing the ability to shift fingers into a new position smoothly without accenting notes that fall on weaker beats. Both of these extroverted solos build technical security and musical confidence.

It is tempting to play *La Gracieuse* slower than the tempo and notation dictate. Because the melody is so graceful, the 32nd-notes are often played more like 16th notes. Careful practice with a metronome will help students hear the faster tempo, and they should be encouraged to perform this study at the correct tempo after they have learned to play the turns with ease. A faster overall tempo is the key here to an effective *leggiero* style.

Inquiétude's challenge lies in playing the alternating left-to-right-hand motives quietly, rapidly, and evenly. The unusual structure of the melody is worth noting. Intermediate students almost exclusively encounter melodies that are quite lyrical, or at least have a distinct, predictable melodic line. This study does not. Its melody is comprised of strings of short, crisp motives that agitate restlessly between the hands. This quality makes it a valuable solo for advancing students to master. Good harmonic understanding will give the piece shape and forward motion, and is crucial to a polished performance. This study will challenge younger students, but their efforts will be amply rewarded—it is an excellent recital showpiece.

L'Adieu is really a wonderful *tarantella*, masquerading as a dramatic, expressive ballad. The sweeping introduction is more effective with an expressive use of *rubato* at its high point. The RH melody's subtle phrasing, coupled with the *allegro molto agitato* tempo, requires fluid technical control. The breaks in the phrases need to be carefully observed, with an audible distinction between the overlapped slurs (see mm. 5-6) and others that break completely (mm. 7-8). The overlapped slurs require little more than a slight lift of the hand, almost like a short intake of breath, to be played with just the right finesse. The LH phrasing is equally important. Observing these breaks throughout gives the constant *legato* melody depth and detail, and imparts an air of breathless excitement to the study.

Embedded melodies are the technical focus of *Le Courant Limpide* and *Consolation*. Of the two, the former is more challenging, although it is placed earlier in the book. Its rapid tempo and *piano* dynamic throughout require very fine finger-control. The embedded melody is found only in the RH and must be brought out without heavy accents, while the accompaniment remains in the background as a quiet, constant murmur. In *Consolation*, both hands are given embedded melodies, although never at the same time.

L'Harmonie des Anges and *L'Hirondelle* focus on playing a smooth, continuous *legato* between the hands. The tempo is fairly moderate in the first of these studies, allowing a performer to shape each phrase in a graceful, expressive arc. *L'Hirondelle* adds the challenge of playing a cross-hand melody smoothly while maintaining a continuous *legato* throughout. Blending notes and matching dynamics from hand to hand are essential to a successful performance. In both studies, awareness of the overall harmonic framework will help students shape the long phrases accurately, and using the damper pedal freely will enhance the overall sound.

Finally, there are the four vivid "character studies" —*La Bergeronnette*, *La Styrienne*, *La Babillarde*, and *Chevaleresque*. These sophisticated, captivating solos deserve a more frequent hearing on recital programs. Their technical demands touch upon a wide variety of skills, but their true focus is musical. Each one has a well-defined, stylized character, sculpted with broad musical gestures. In recital, it is actually quite helpful to imagine an actor appearing onstage. They are true musical portraits, and should be performed with great flair.

La Bergeronnette is insouciant and flirtatious; *La Babillarde* is a deftly humorous musical portrait of a young chatterbox. *La Styrienne* is a playful, robust dance. Its 3/4 meter and sturdy, accented downbeats recall the Austrian folk dance, the Ländler. Indeed, *La Styrienne* is appropriately translated as *Austrian Dance*. Styria is a province in southeastern Austria which was established in the 12th century. The Ländler is one of its many traditional folk dances. *Chevaleresque*'s jaunty, fearlessly confident style aptly conjures up a gallant knight on horseback. This last character piece ends the collection with a virtuoso flourish.

—*Margaret Otwell*

La Candeur

Sincerity

J. Friedrich Burgmüller
Op. 100, No. 1

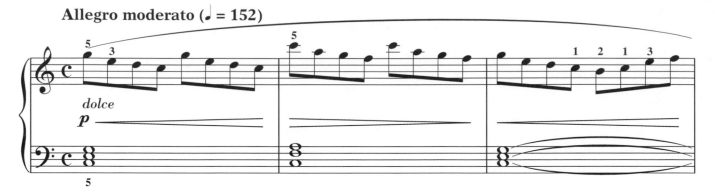

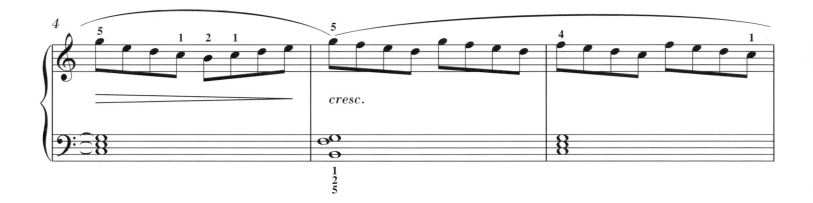

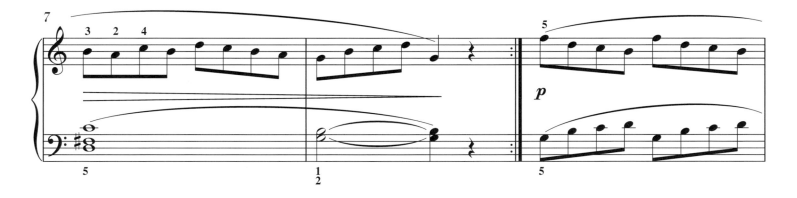

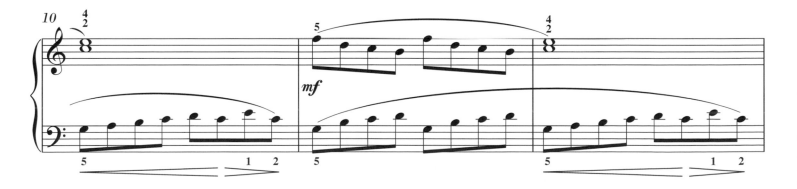

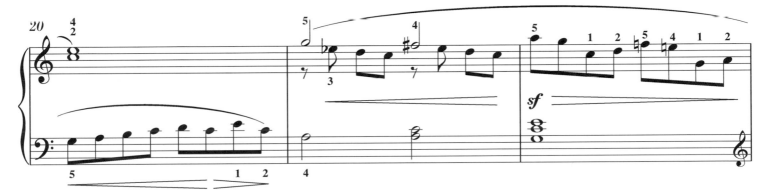

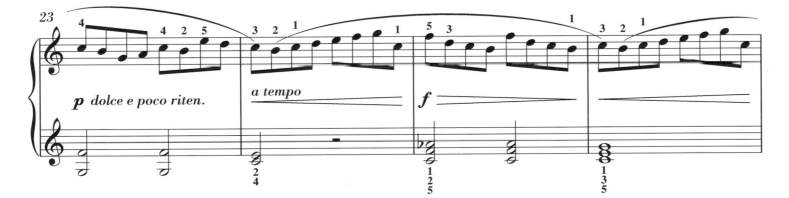

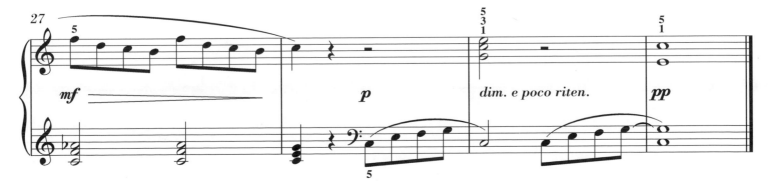

L'Arabesque
Arabesque

J. Friedrich Burgmüller
Op. 100, No. 2

Allegro scherzando (♩ = 152)

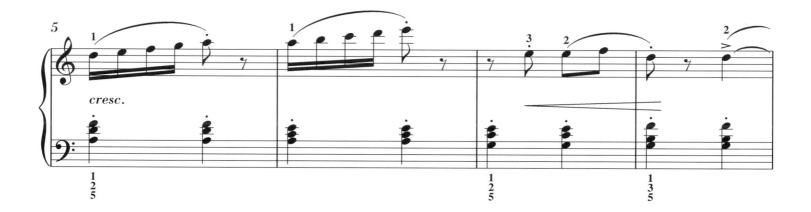

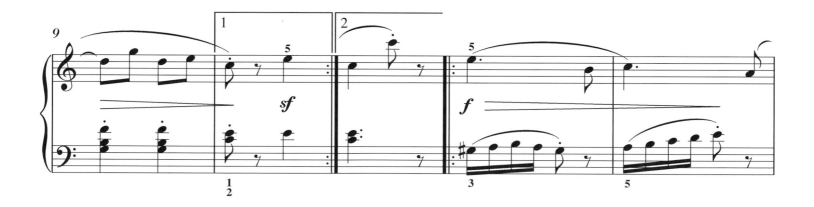

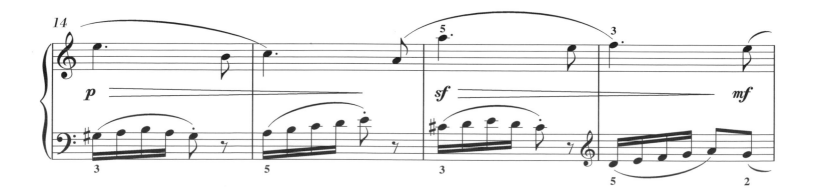

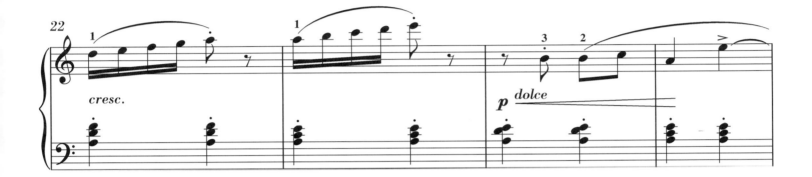

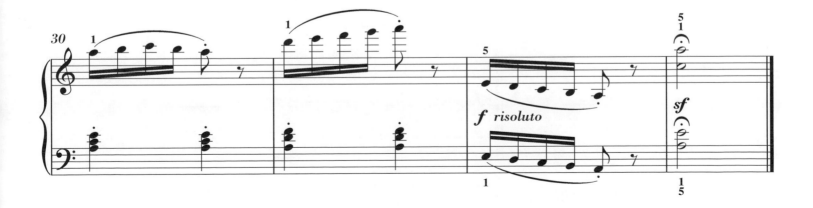

La Pastorale

Pastorale

J. Friedrich Burgmüller
Op. 100, No. 3

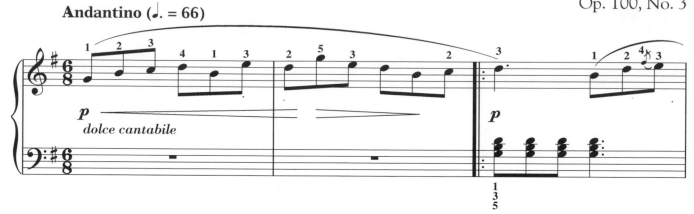

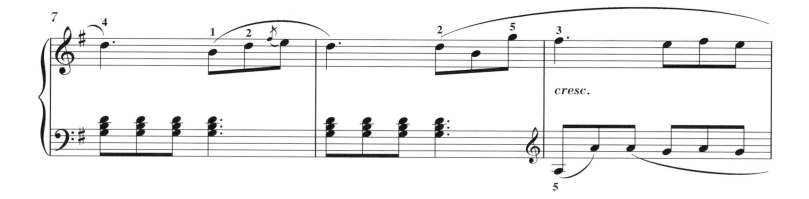

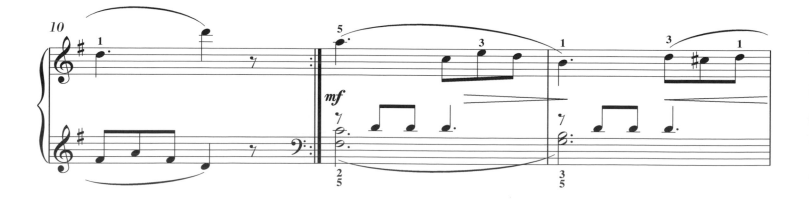

La Petite Réunion

The Little Party

J. Friedrich Burgmüller
Op. 100, No. 4

Allegro non troppo (♩ = 152)

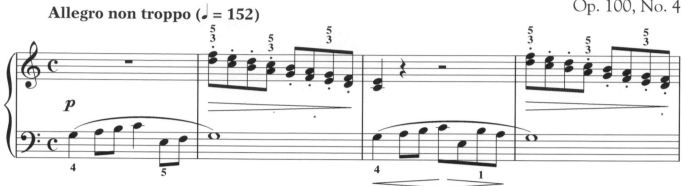

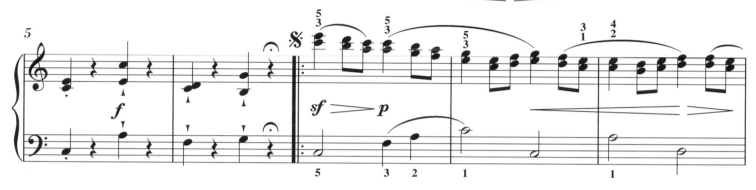

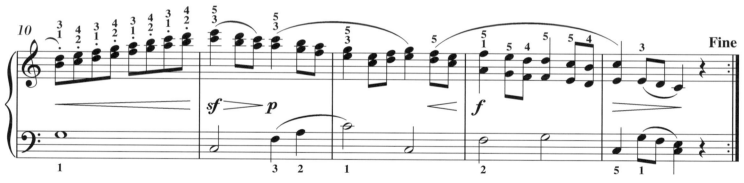

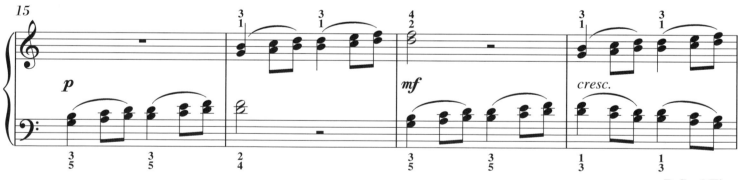

D.S. al Fine
senza repetizione

Innocence

J. Friedrich Burgmüller
Op. 100, No. 5

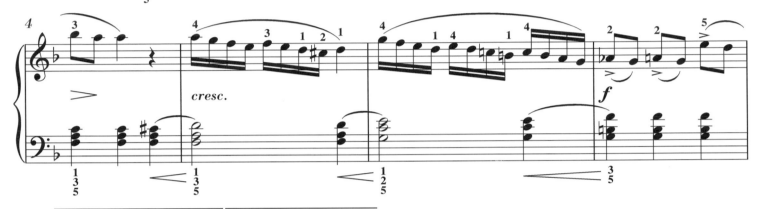

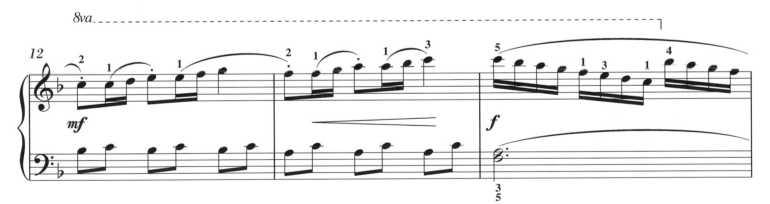

Progrès
Progress

J. Friedrich Burgmüller
Op. 100, No. 6

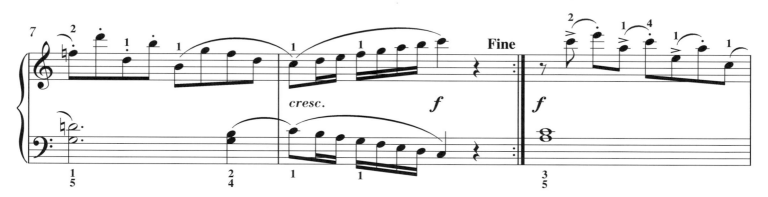
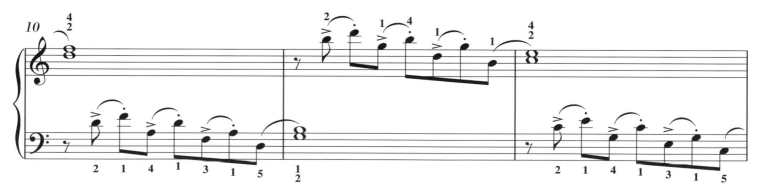
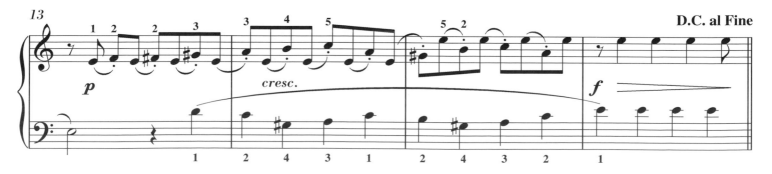

Le Courant Limpide
The Limpid Stream

J. Friedrich Burgmüller
Op. 100, No. 7

Allegro vivace (♩ = 176)

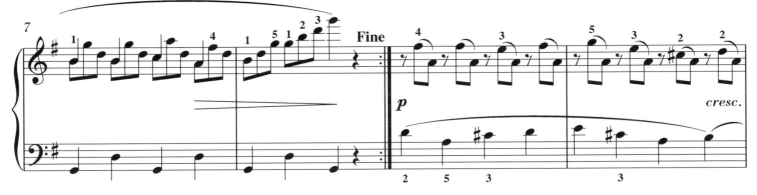

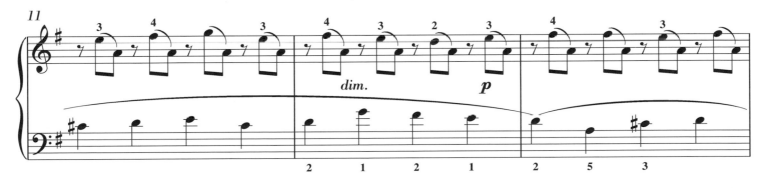

La Gracieuse
Gracefulness

J. Friedrich Burgmüller
Op. 100, No. 8

La Chasse
The Chase

J. Friedrich Burgmüller
Op. 100, No. 9

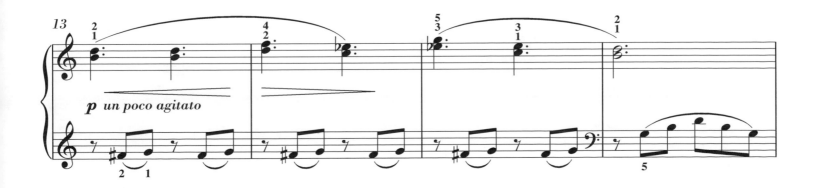

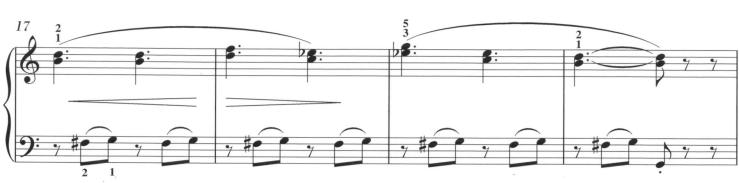

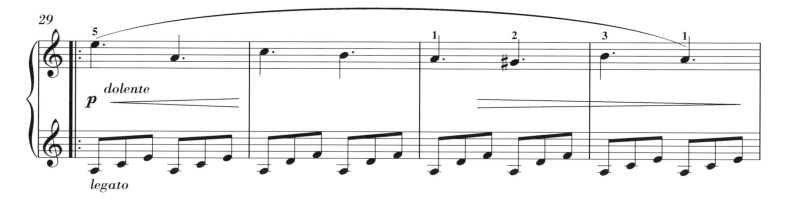

Tendre Fleur
Tender Flower

J. Friedrich Burgmüller
Op. 100, No. 10

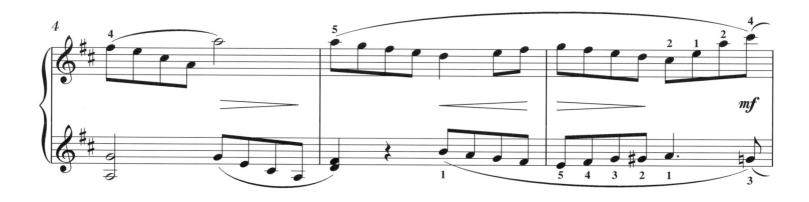

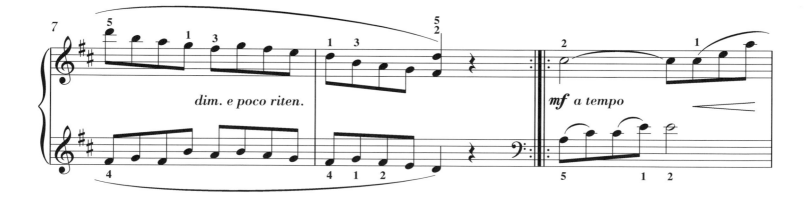

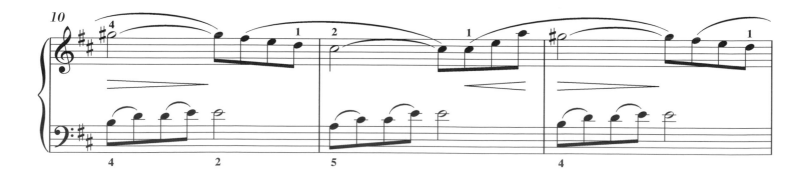

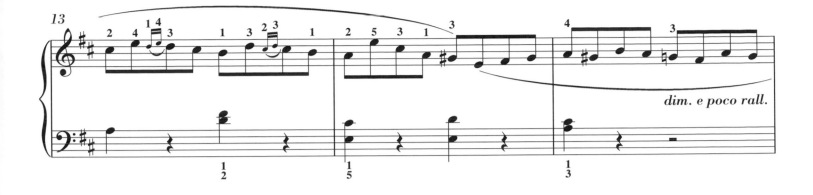

La Bergeronnette

The Young Shepherdess

J. Friedrich Burgmüller
Op. 100, No. 11

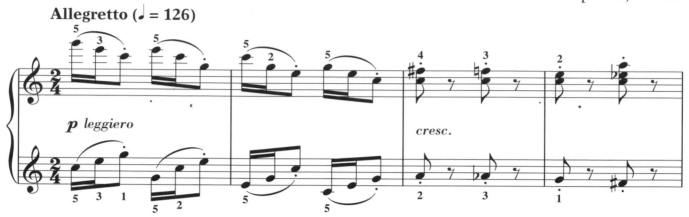

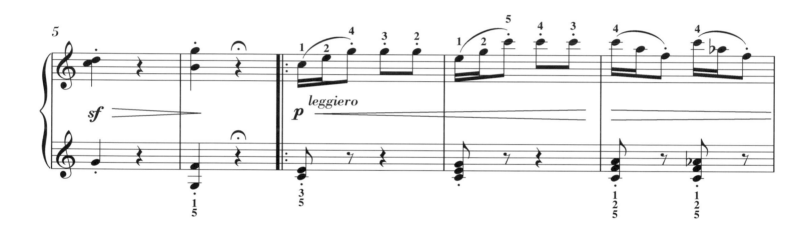

L'Adieu
The Farewell

J. Friedrich Burgmüller
Op. 100, No. 12

Allegro molto agitato (♩ = 184)

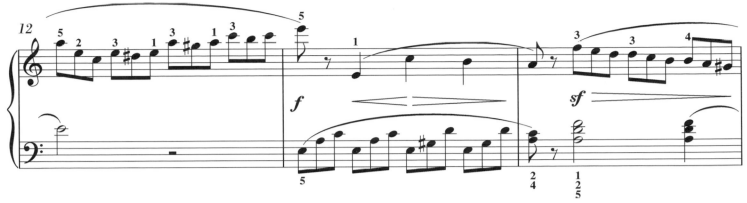

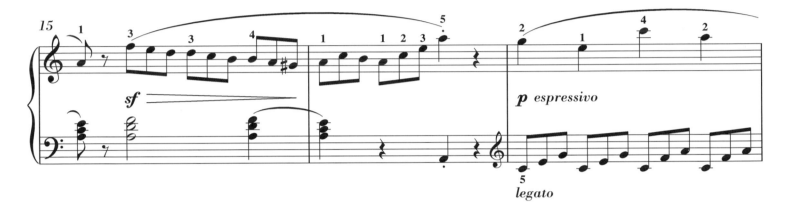

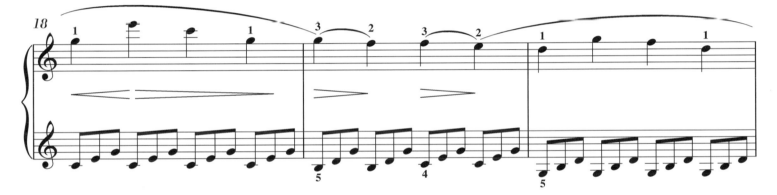

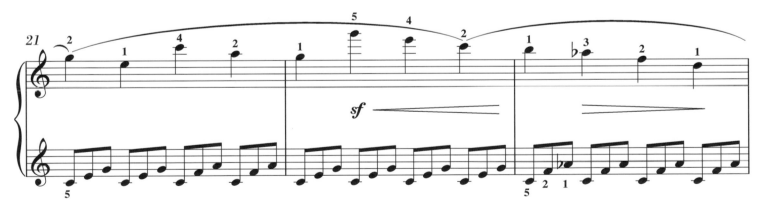

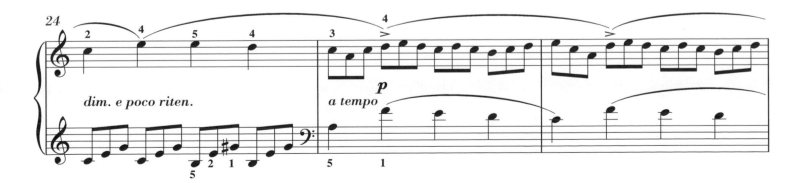

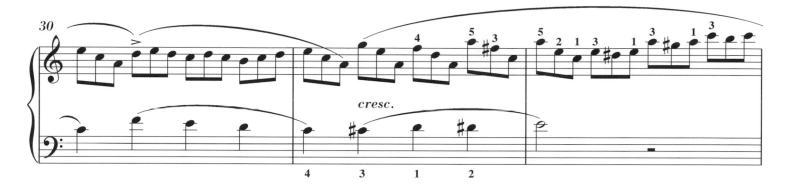

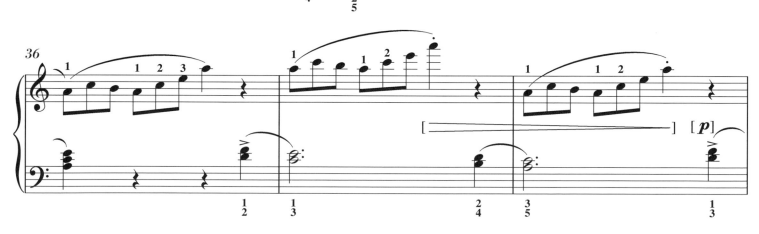

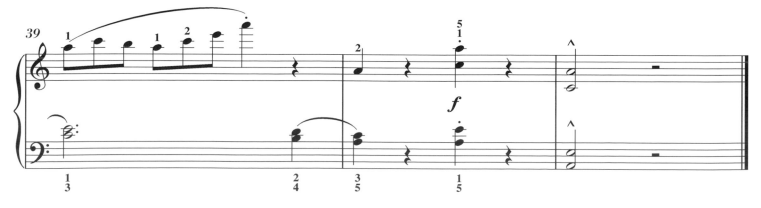

Consolation

J. Friedrich Burgmüller
Op. 100, No. 13

Allegro moderato (♩ = 152)

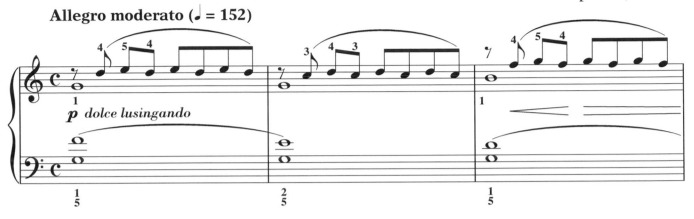

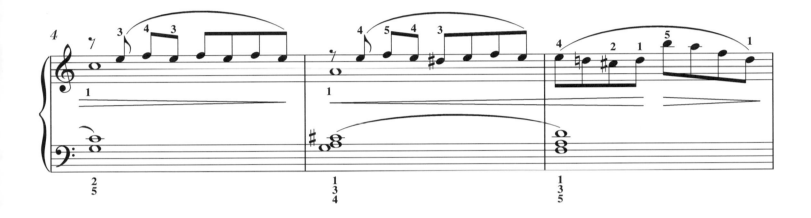

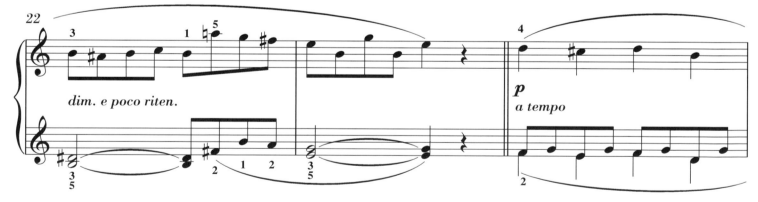

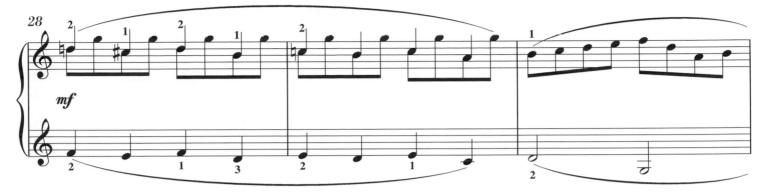

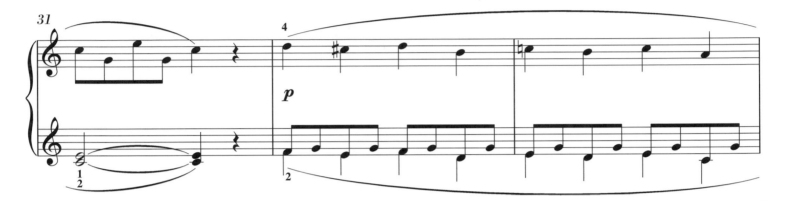

La Styrienne

Austrian Dance

J. Friedrich Burgmüller
Op. 100, No. 14

Mouvement de Valse (♩ = 176)

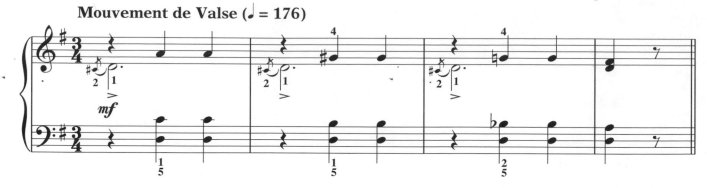

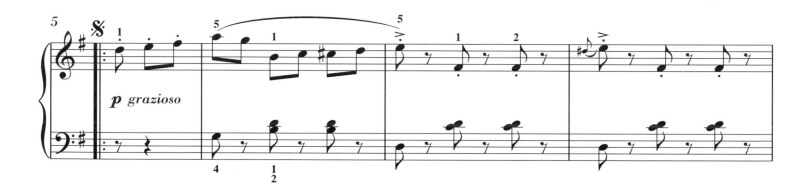

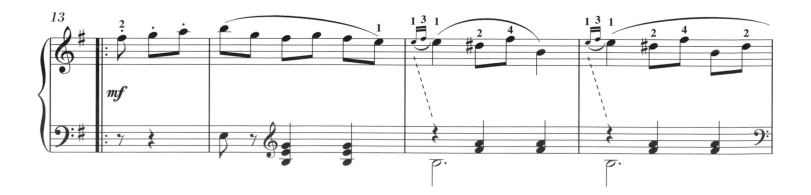

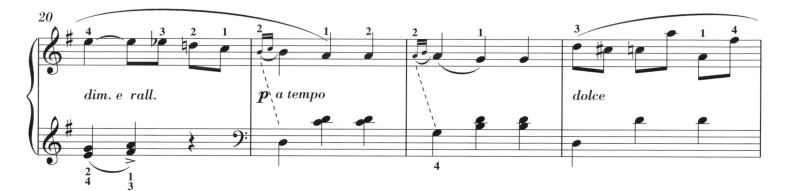

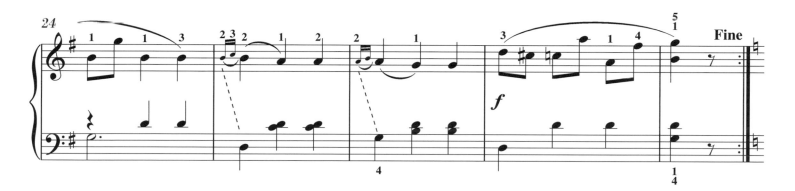

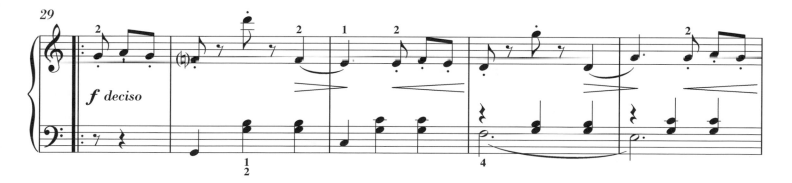

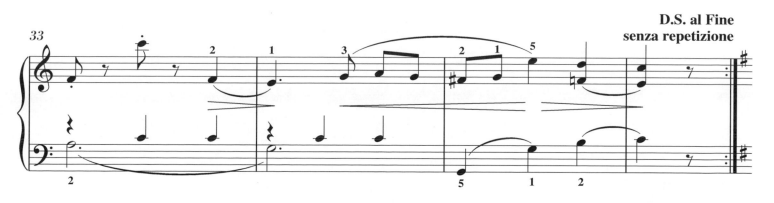

Ballade

J. Friedrich Burgmüller
Op. 100, No. 15

Allegro con brio (♩. = 104)

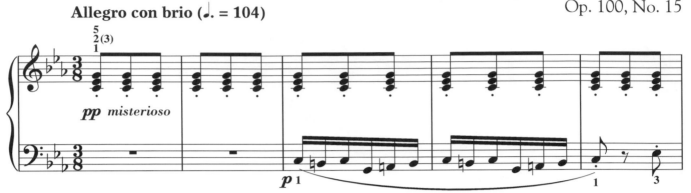

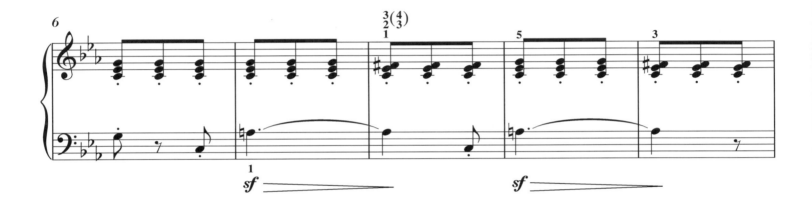

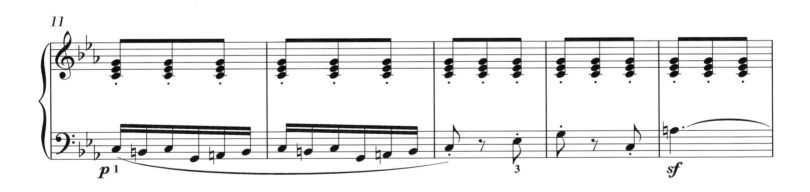

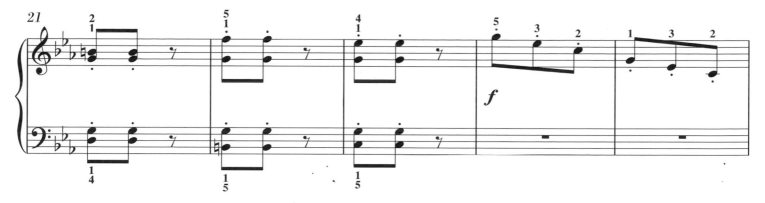

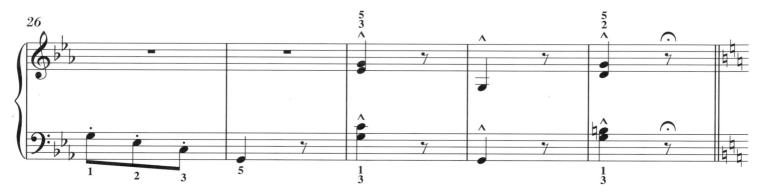

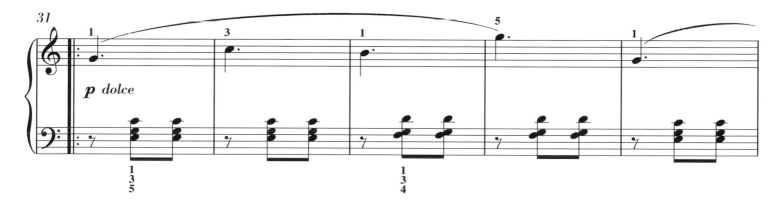

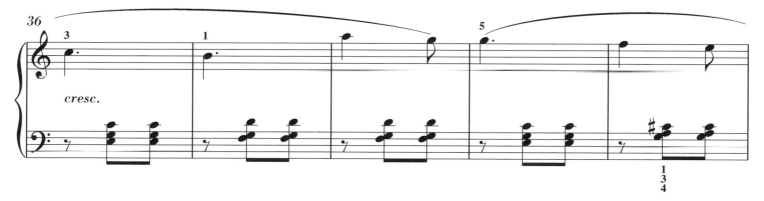

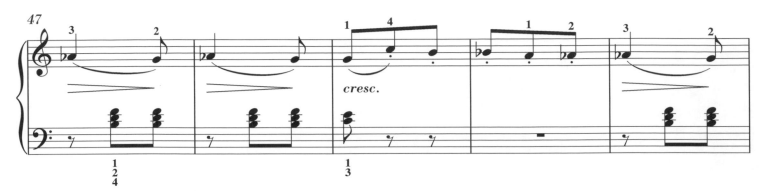

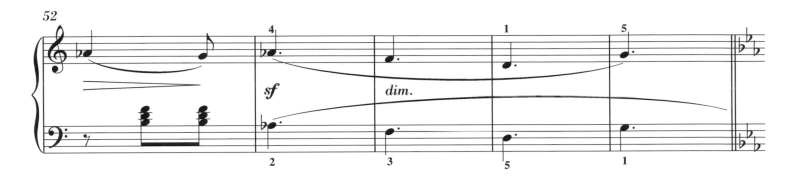

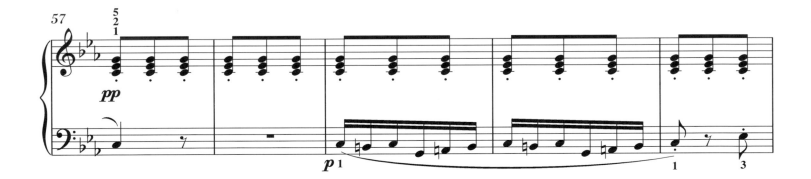

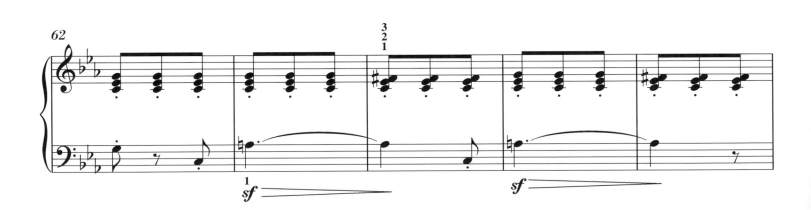

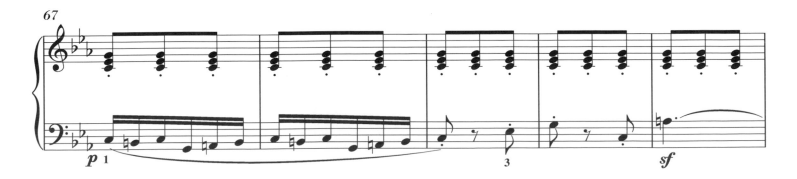

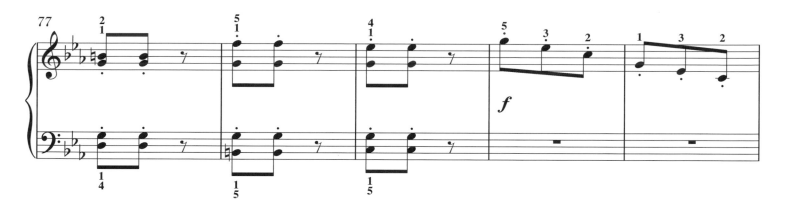

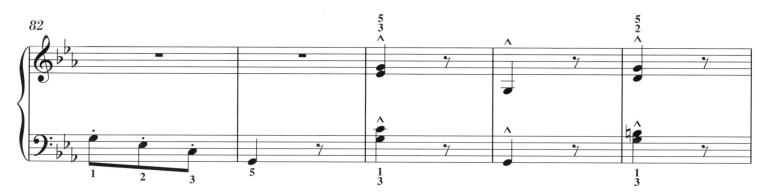

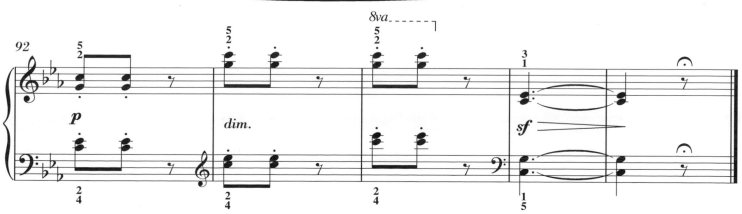

Douce Plainte
Gentle Lament

J. Friedrich Burgmüller
Op. 100, No. 16

Allegro moderato (♩ = 126)

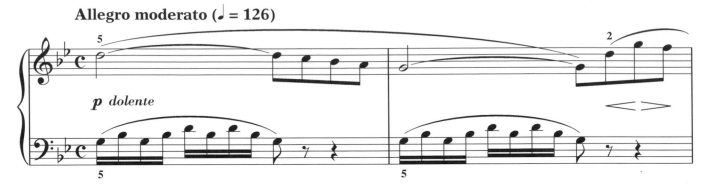

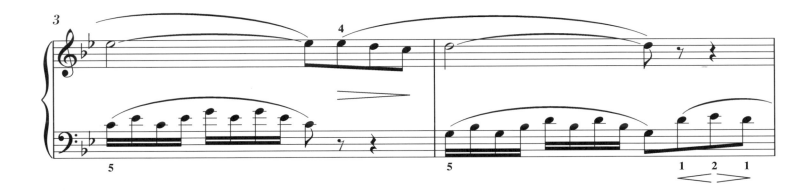

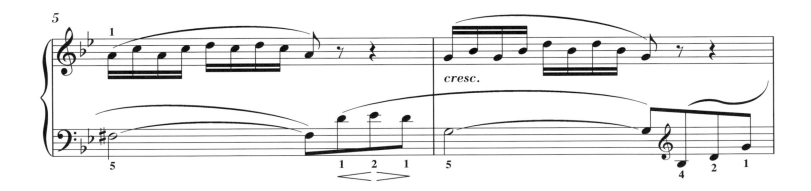

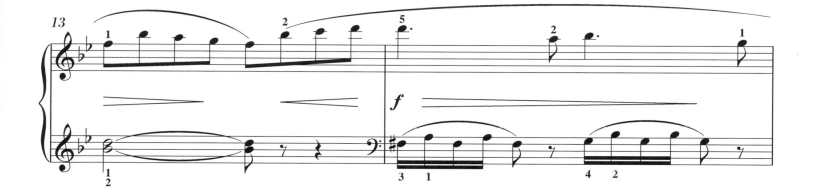

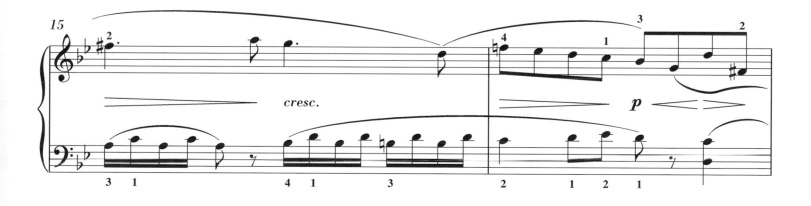

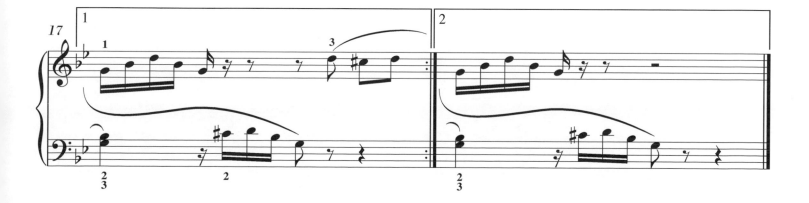

La Babillarde

The Chatterbox

J. Friedrich Burgmüller
Op. 100, No. 17

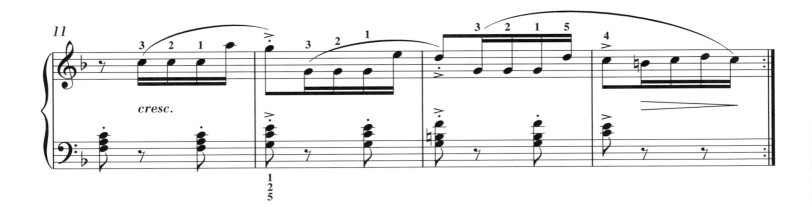

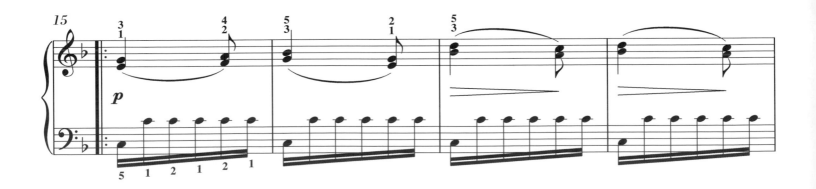

Inquiétude

Restlessness

J. Friedrich Burgmüller
Op. 100, No. 18

Ave Maria

J. Friedrich Burgmüller
Op. 100, No. 19

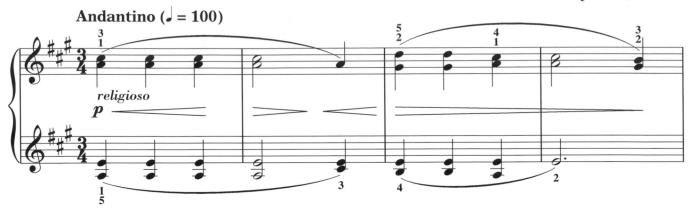

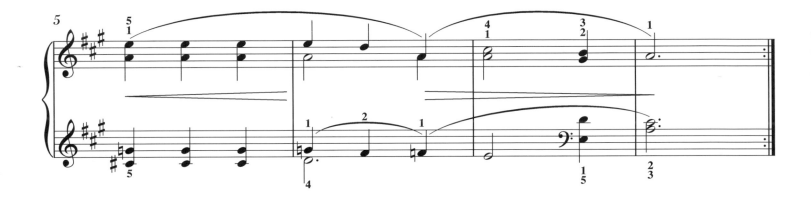

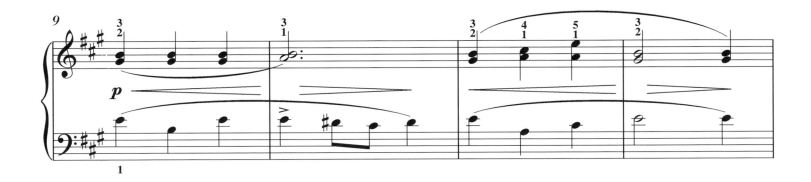

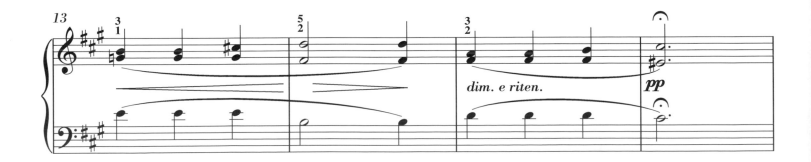

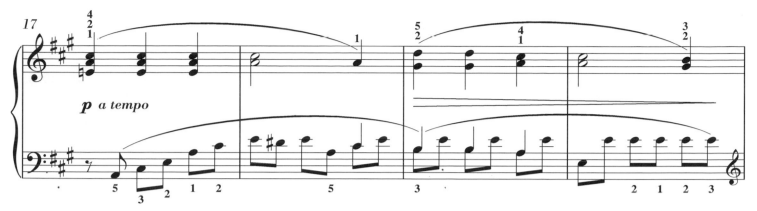

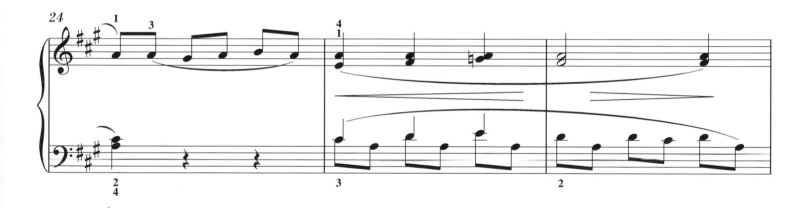

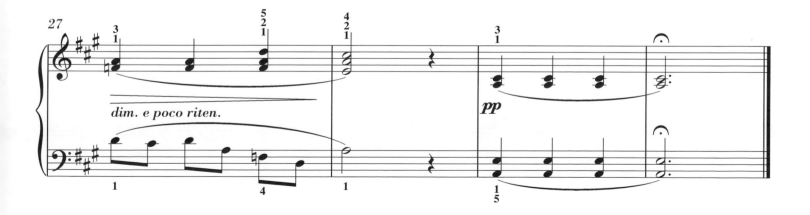

La Tarentelle
Tarantella

J. Friedrich Burgmüller
Op. 100, No. 20

Allegro vivo (♩. = 160)

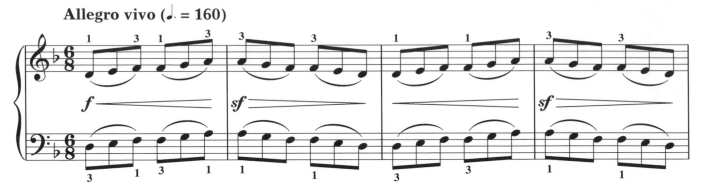

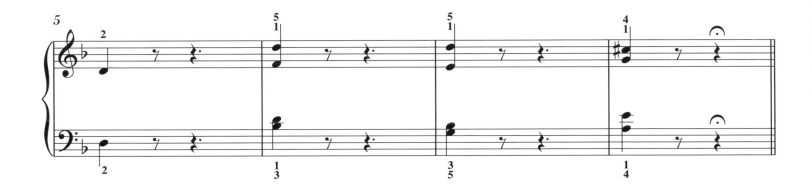

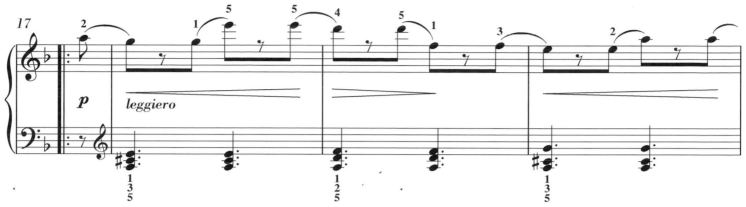

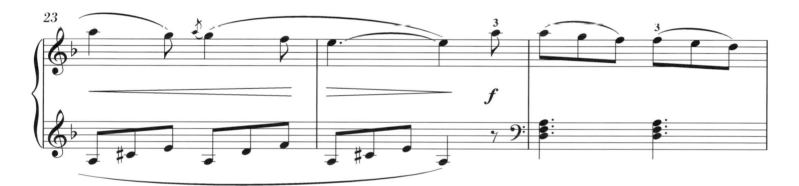

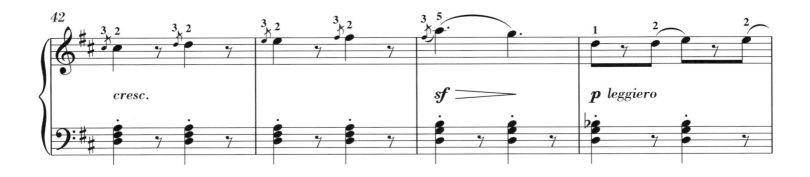

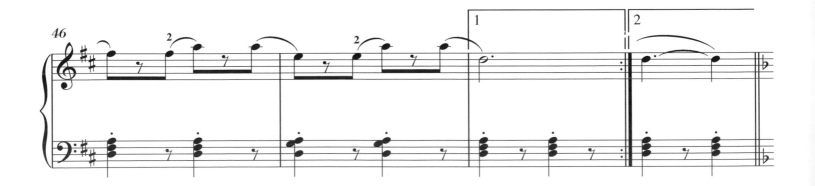

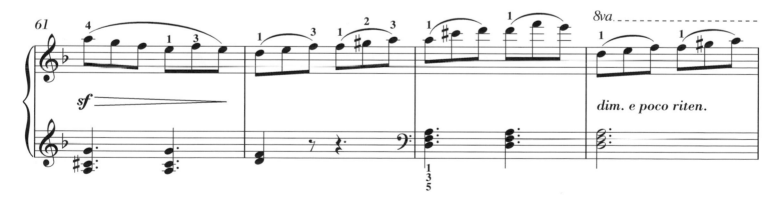

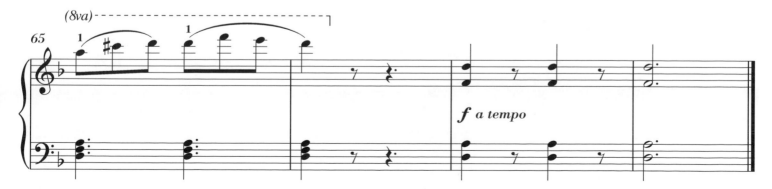

L'Harmonie des Anges

The Harmony of the Angels

J. Friedrich Burgmüller
Op. 100, No. 21

Allegro moderato (♩ = 152)

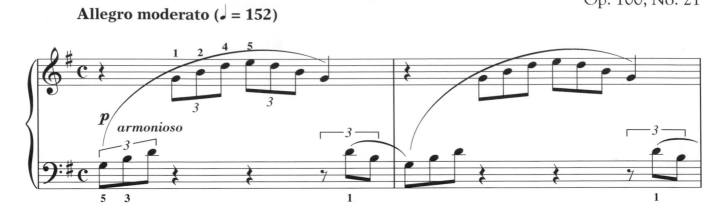

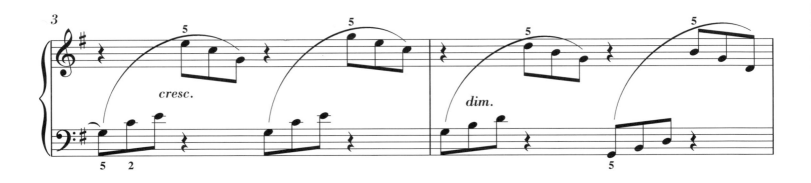

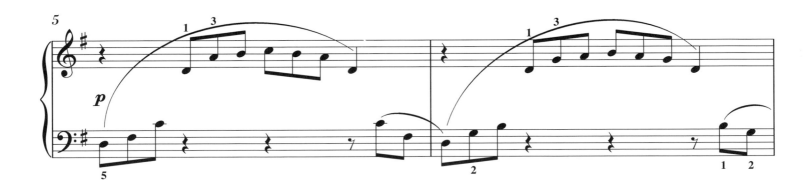

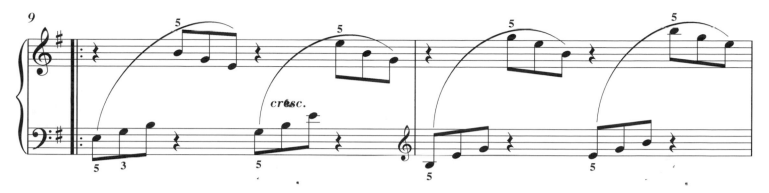

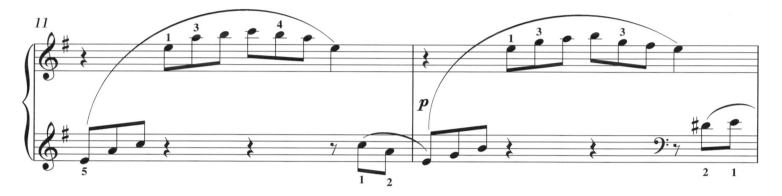

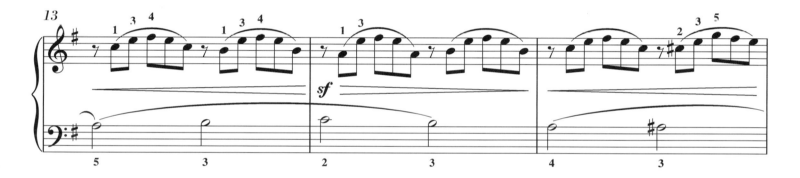

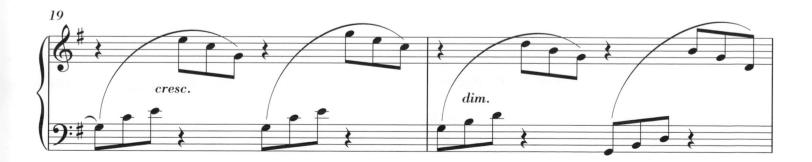

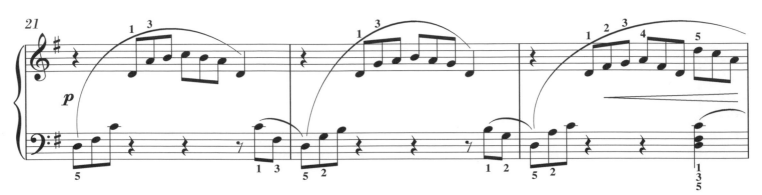

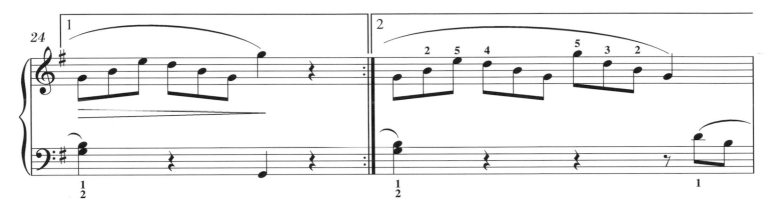

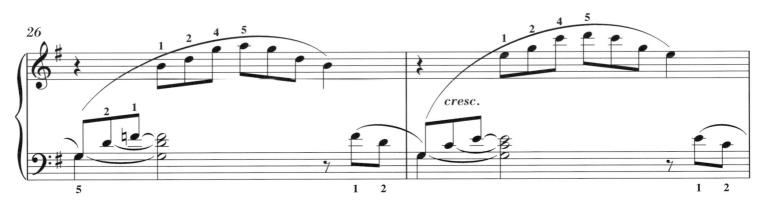

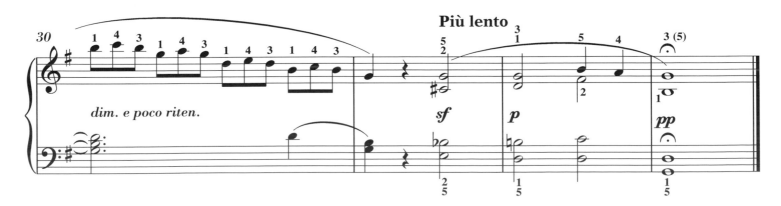

Barcarolle

J. Friedrich Burgmüller
Op. 100, No. 22

Andantino quasi allegretto ($\quad$ = 72)

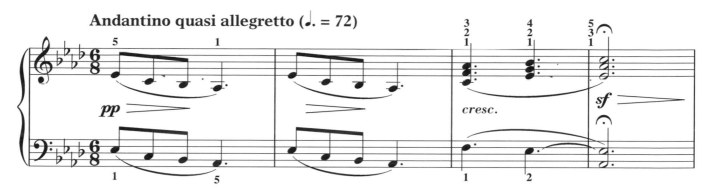

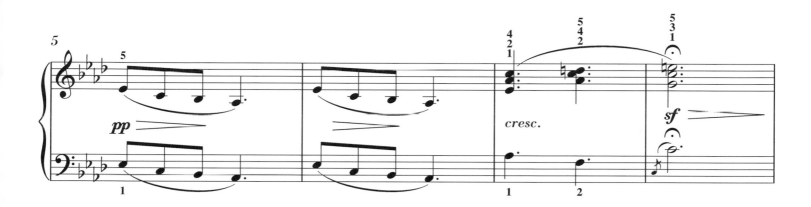

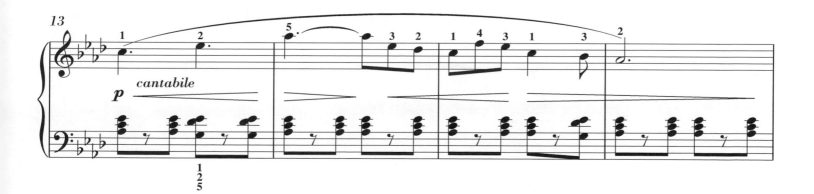

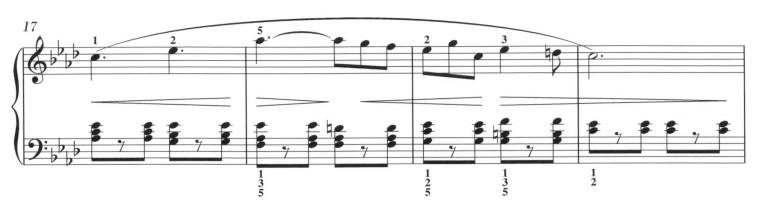

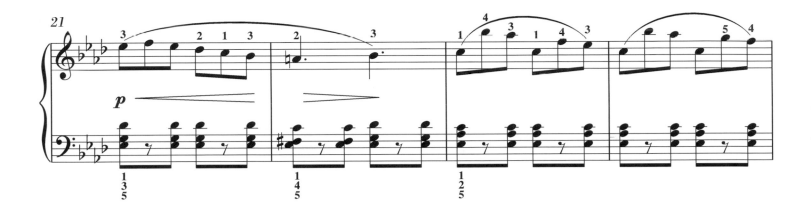

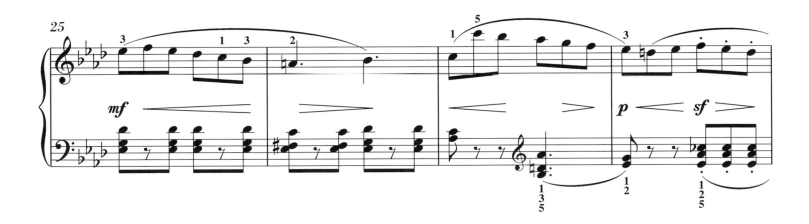

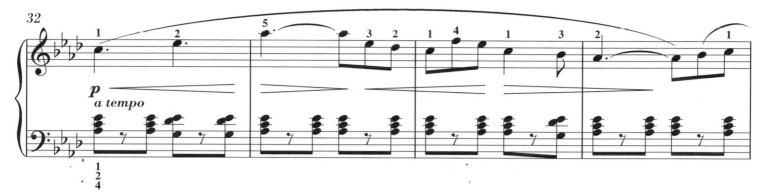

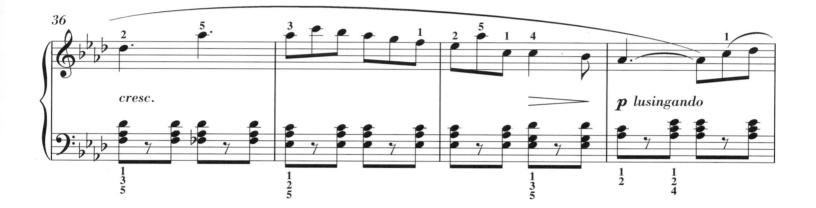

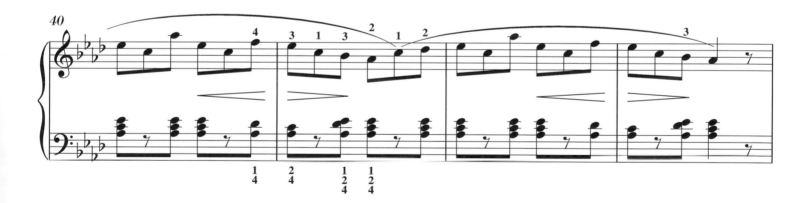

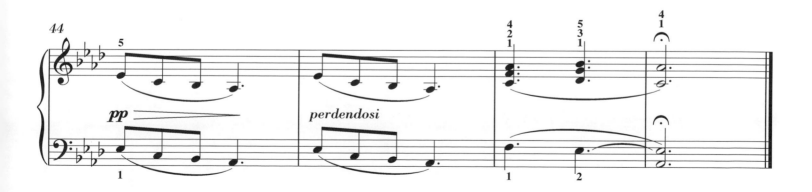

Le Retour
The Return

J. Friedrich Burgmüller
Op. 100, No. 23

Molto agitato quasi presto (♩. = 126)

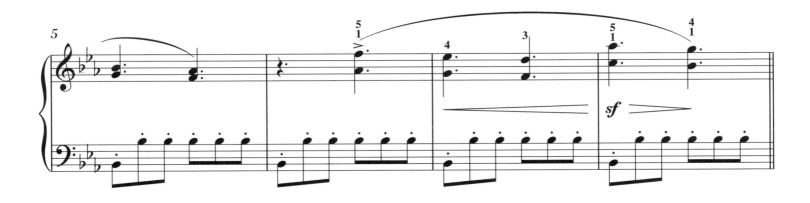

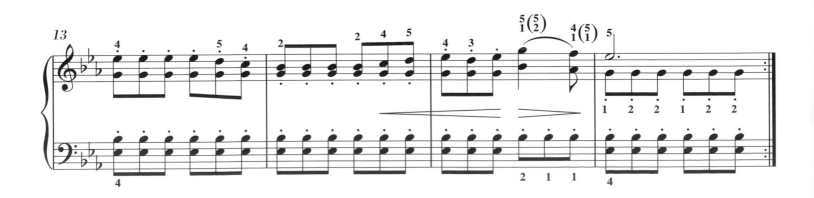

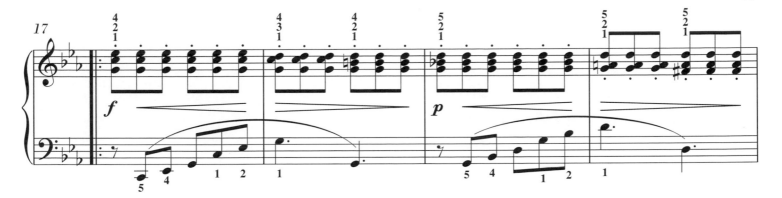

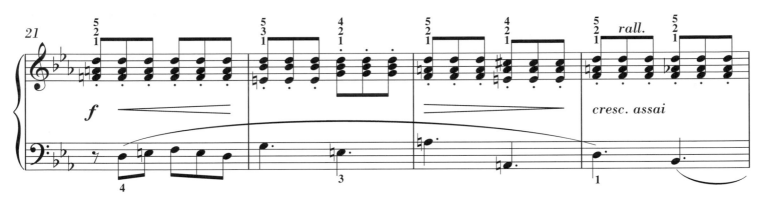

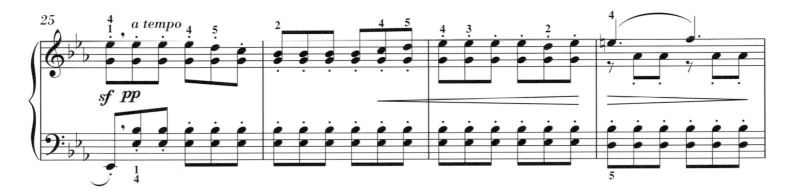

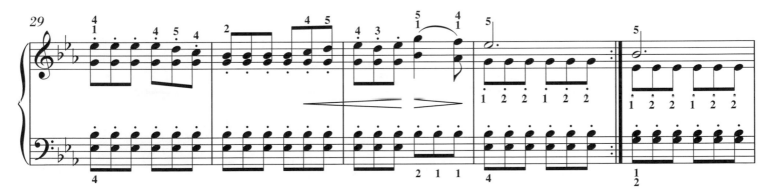

L'Hirondelle
The Swallow

J. Friedrich Burgmüller
Op. 100, No. 24

Allegro non troppo (♩ = 138)

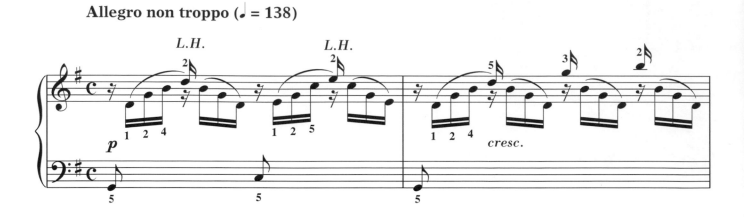

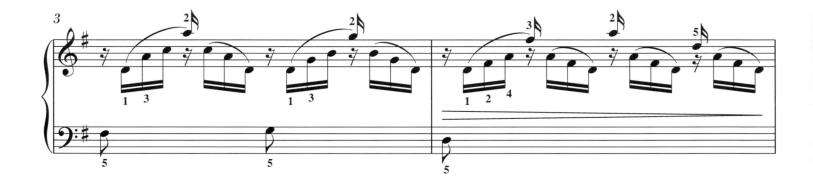

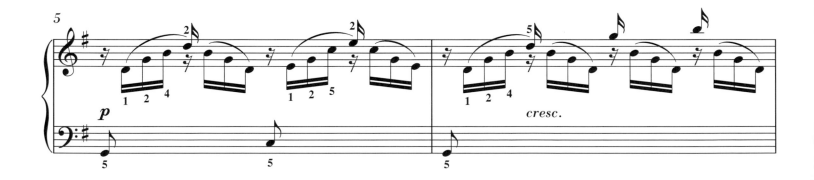

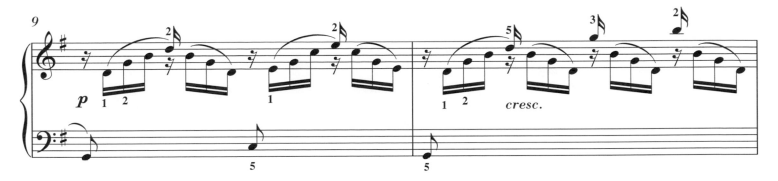
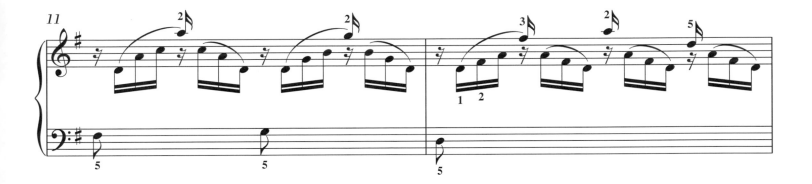
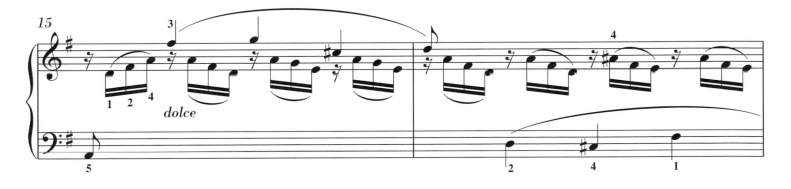
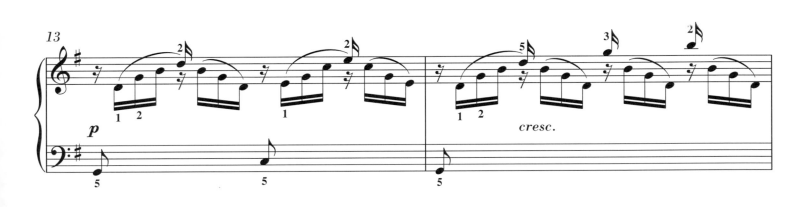
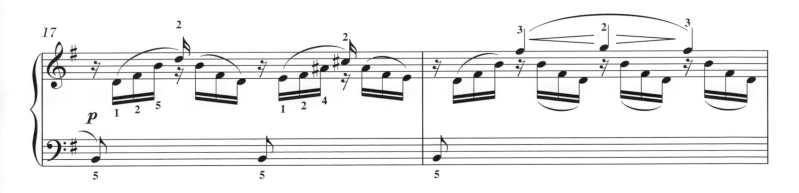

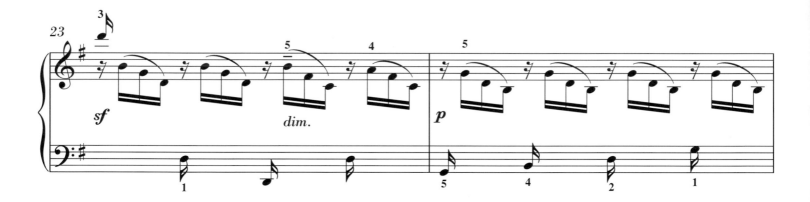

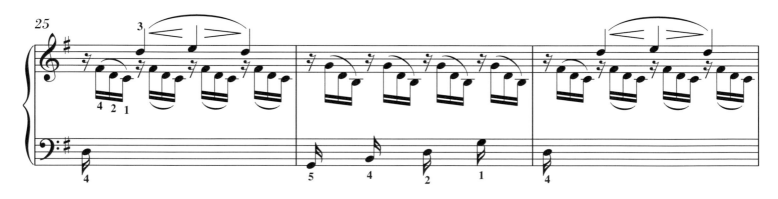

Chevaleresque
Gallantry

J. Friedrich Burgmüller
Op. 100, No. 25

Allegro marziale (♩ = 152)

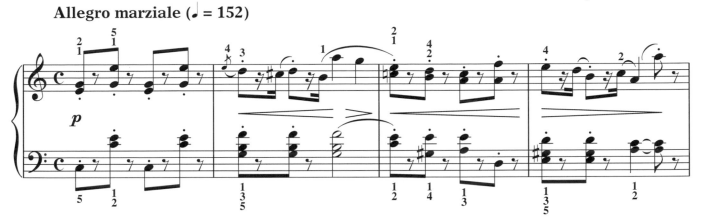

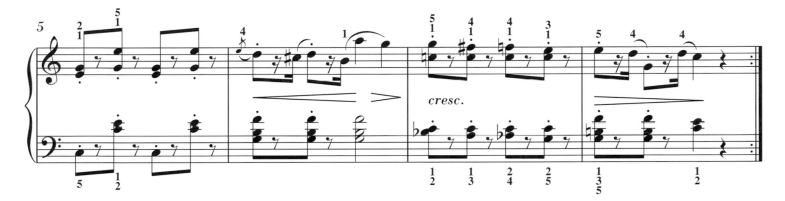

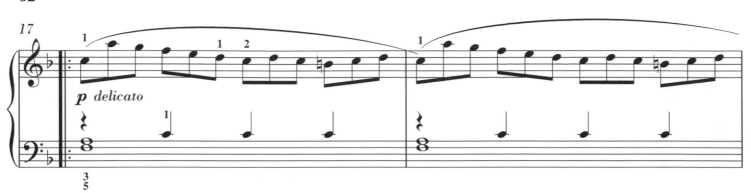

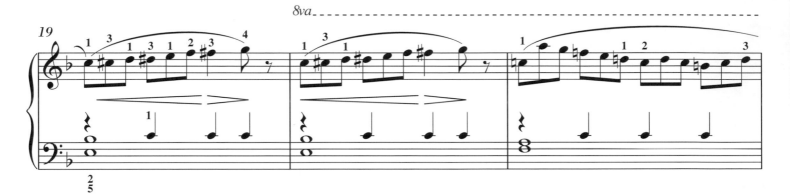

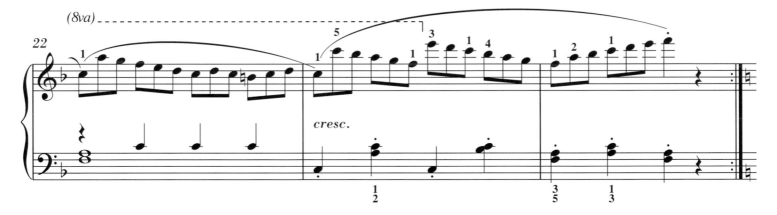

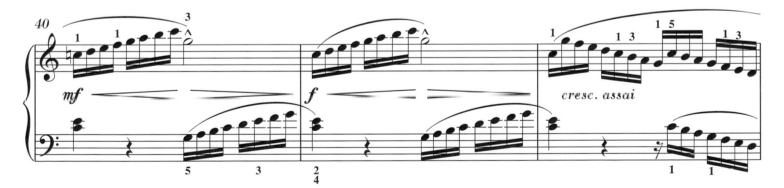

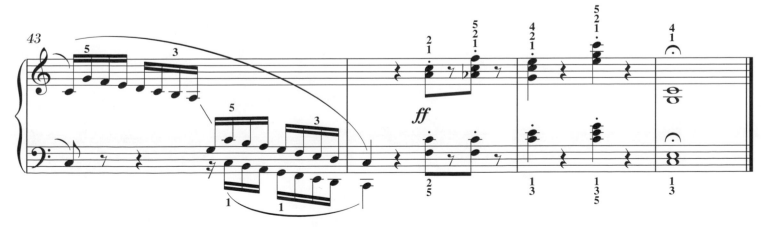

ABOUT THE EDITOR

MARGARET OTWELL

Margaret Otwell is a musician with a distinguished and varied career as a solo pianist, collaborative musician, and teacher. She has pursued an active role in educating young pianists as an independent piano teacher for over 25 years. A member of MTNA since 1978, she is a past president of the Northern Virginia Music Teachers Association, and has adjudicated for many piano competitions and events, including the Wolf Trap Young Artist Competition in Washington, DC and the National Piano Arts Competition in Milwaukee. Dr. Otwell has served on the faculties of the University of Maryland Eastern Shore, The American University Preparatory Department, and George Mason University. She is currently Director of Educational Keyboard Publications for Hal Leonard Corporation in Milwaukee, WI.

As a pianist, Dr. Otwell is well-known for her insightful interpretation of French piano repertoire. She has recorded the complete works of Déodat de Séverac for Musical Heritage Society Records. She has presented lecture-recitals, workshops, and master classes and has appeared in solo and chamber music performances throughout the United States, Canada, and Europe. Dr. Otwell was awarded a DMA degree in Performance from the University of Maryland, where she studied piano and pedagogy with Stewart Gordon, Thomas Schumacher, and Nelita True. She also studied piano with Gaby Casadesus as a recipient of a Fulbright performance grant to France.